THE STORY KEEPERS

The COMPLETE
STORYKEEPERS
COLLECTION

Brian Brown and Andrew Melrose

hunt &
thorpe

Hunt & Thorpe
Hunt & Thorpe is an imprint of
Paternoster Publishing,
P.O. Box 300, Kingstown Broadway, Carlisle, Cumbria CA3 0QS, UK.

Designed by Tony Cantale Graphics.

Originally published as individual episodes in the UK by
Cassell, Wellington House, 125 Strand, London WC2R 0BB, 1996–1998.

British Library Cataloguing-in-Publication Data
A catalogue record for this book is available from the British Library.

ISBN 1-85608-395-0

Printed in Singapore by Star Standard Industries Pte. Ltd.

Contents

Look out for these characters

Cyrus

Tacticus

Nero

Mordecai

Hadrian

4

Milo

The lion cubs

Flavian

Capella

Miriam

Nihilus

5

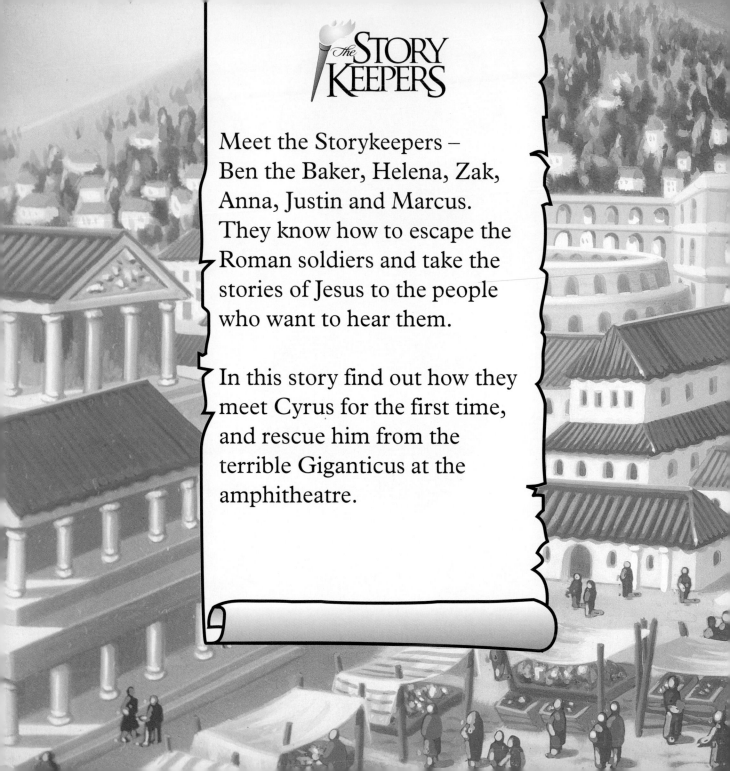

Meet the Storykeepers –
Ben the Baker, Helena, Zak,
Anna, Justin and Marcus.
They know how to escape the
Roman soldiers and take the
stories of Jesus to the people
who want to hear them.

In this story find out how they
meet Cyrus for the first time,
and rescue him from the
terrible Giganticus at the
amphitheatre.

The STORY KEEPERS

Episode 1

Breakout!

Long ago, in the city of Rome,
there lived a mighty ruler.
His name was Nero.
He thought he was a god,
but the Christians knew he wasn't.
So Nero hated them.

One day there was a great fire.
Nero said the Christians started it,
and he sent his cruel soldiers after them.

Marcus, Justin, and Anna
lost their parents during the fire.
Ben the baker and his wife, Helena,
took them into their home.
There, in a time of great danger,
they told the children stories about Jesus.

This book is about the adventures
of the Storykeepers.

The STORY KEEPERS

"Bread! Freshly baked bread!" Ben shouted.
"Bread for sale," Helena called.

| Ben | Helena | Zak | Justin | Anna | Marcus |

Ben was the best baker in Rome.
Helena was his wife.
Ben and Helena were Christians.
They took care of Zak, Justin, Anna, and Marcus.

The children watched a juggler.
His name was Cyrus.
"How do you do that?" Anna cried.
"Let me show you," said Cyrus.

Anna and Cyrus soon became friends.
"Come to our secret meeting tonight," Anna told Cyrus.
"Ben is going to tell a story about Jesus."

Later that day, Cyrus and the children
went to the secret meeting.
It was dangerous.
The Romans did not want anyone
to tell stories about Jesus.
But Ben loved Jesus.
He wanted to tell the children about him.

"My father was a baker like me,"
Ben told the children.
"One day, I went to hear Jesus preach.
My father gave me a lunch to take with me."

Many people came to hear Jesus.
Over five thousand of them!
Jesus talked to them until it began to get dark.
Everyone was hungry.

"How much food can you find?"
Jesus asked his friends.
"Only five loaves and two fishes," his friends replied.
And they pointed at Ben.

Jesus took the bread and gave thanks to God. Then he broke it into bits, and his friends passed the bread to the people.

Everyone had enough to eat!
They even filled twelve baskets with leftover food.

Suddenly, there was a banging on the door.
It was the soldiers!
"Open up!" they ordered.

"Hurry!" Ben called to the children. Ben, Helena, and the children escaped through a secret exit in the floor.

But Cyrus, the juggler, fell behind. The soldiers caught him and took him away.

The children were very upset.
"We must rescue Cyrus!" they said to Ben.
Ben had an idea.
"We will deliver bread to the prison," he told them.
"Then we will find out where Cyrus is."

Ben, Helena, and the children found Cyrus. "There he is!" Anna cried.

"Are you scared, Cyrus?" Anna asked.
"Yes," Cyrus replied. "Tomorrow I have to fight Giganticus. He's huge, and I am small!"

"Zacchaeus was a little man, too,
but he was brave," Helena said.
And she told Cyrus a story
to cheer him up.

Everyone hated Zacchaeus
because he was a tax collector.
He was rich, but did not have any friends.

One day, Zacchaeus heard that Jesus was coming.
Zacchaeus really wanted to see Jesus.
But he was too small.
He climbed a tree so he could see.

Jesus saw Zacchaeus in the tree. "Zacchaeus!" he called. "Come down! I must stay in your house today!"

This made the people angry. "Zacchaeus is a thief and a cheat!" they shouted.

Jesus smiled.
He went to Zacchaeus's house.
He stayed all afternoon.
Zacchaeus was so happy!
"I will give money to the poor,"
he told Jesus. "And I will pay back
all the people I have cheated."

While Stouticus was eating cakes,
Marcus crept up behind him.
He made a print of Stouticus's
key in some dough.
Then Ben and the gang hurried
back to the bakery.

Ben baked a special hard
biscuit in the shape of the key
to Cyrus's cell!

The next day, Ben and Zak returned to the prison.
They took along Ben's special key.
Ben gave cakes to the guards to keep them busy.
And Zak used the key to open Cyrus's cell!

"Follow me," Zak whispered.
He pointed to a door ahead.
Bright sunlight streamed under the door.

Cyrus and the other prisoners followed Zak.
They opened the door.
They blinked in the strong sunlight.
They heard shouting and cheering.

Then they saw him.
Giganticus!
They had walked right into the arena.

"Leave it to me," Cyrus said.
And he began to juggle.
He bounced a helmet
off the giant's head.
The crowd roared.

"Can't catch me!"
Cyrus teased the giant.
Swish! went the huge sword.
Giganticus knocked out Zak.
Then he headed straight
 for Cyrus.
"Can't catch me!"
Cyrus laughed.
Giganticus roared with
anger.

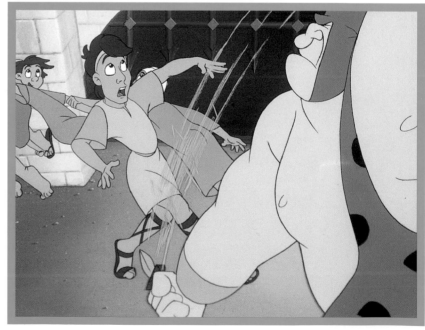

No one noticed
Ben opening a gate.
No one saw Justin
climb into a chariot.

The other Christians escaped through the gate.
But Cyrus and Zak were still trapped!

Justin raced up in the chariot.
He grabbed Cyrus and Zak.

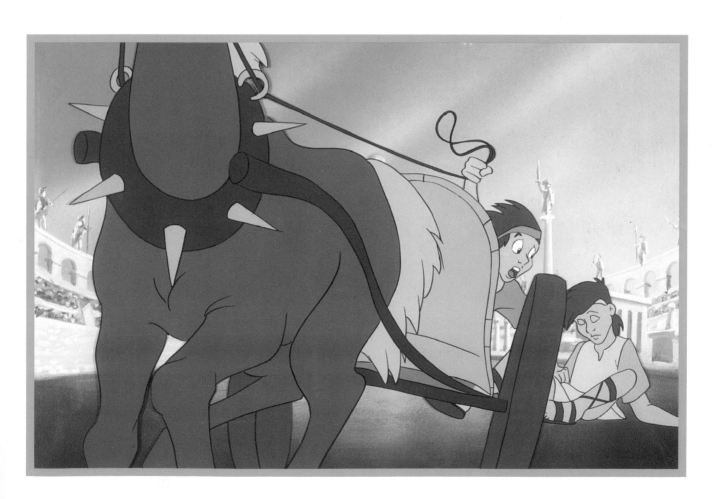

And they escaped through the gate,
too.

Back in the bakery, Ben and the children
celebrated with a big dinner.
"Will you stay with us?" Ben asked Cyrus.
He knew Cyrus would not find his parents.

"Oh, may I?" Cyrus cried.
His eyes shone with happiness.
And all the children cheered.

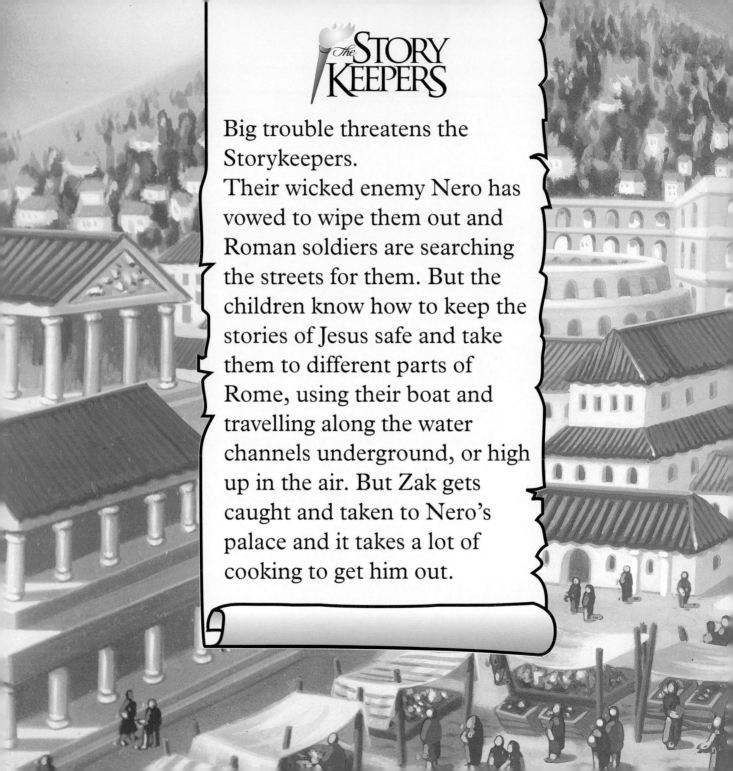

The STORY KEEPERS

Big trouble threatens the Storykeepers. Their wicked enemy Nero has vowed to wipe them out and Roman soldiers are searching the streets for them. But the children know how to keep the stories of Jesus safe and take them to different parts of Rome, using their boat and travelling along the water channels underground, or high up in the air. But Zak gets caught and taken to Nero's palace and it takes a lot of cooking to get him out.

L ong ago, in the city of Rome,
there lived a mighty ruler.
His name was Nero.
He thought he was a god,
but the Christians knew he wasn't.
So Nero hated them.

One day there was a great fire.
Nero said the Christians started it,
and he sent his cruel soldiers after them.

Marcus, Justin, and Anna
lost their parents during the fire.
Ben the baker and his wife, Helena,
took them into their home.
There, in a time of great danger,
they told the children stories about Jesus.

This book is about the adventures
of the Storykeepers.

"Look at this!" Ben called.
He tossed a piece of dough
and balanced it on his nose.
Justin, Anna, and Cyrus laughed.
But Helena was worried.
"Where is Zak?" she asked.
"I hope he is all right."

But Zak wasn't all right.
Soldiers were chasing him,
and he was running for his life.
He ran down the street.
He climbed over walls.
But they cornered him.

Quickly he jumped
onto a horse.
The horse threw him
over a wall into a
fountain.
He ducked under the
water so the soldiers
could not see him.

When the soldiers went away, Zak ran back to the bakery.
"Bad news!" he told Ben and Helena.
"The storykeeper in North Rome was captured!
Who will tell a story to the Christians there tonight?"
"I can't go," said Ben.
"I am telling a story here tonight
about a man called John."

John lived in the desert.
"Someone very important
is coming," he told the people,
"so stop being selfish. Share what you have."
Many of the people wanted to change their ways.
So he baptized them in the river.

Not long after,
Jesus arrived at the river bank.
Just like the others,
Jesus asked John to baptize him.

Then something wonderful happened.
Jesus came up out of the water.
He looked up.
The clouds above him opened.
He heard a voice:
"You are my only Son.
I am pleased with you."

"That's a great story," said Zak,
"but what about the Christians
in North Rome?"
"I have another story for them,"
Ben replied.
He wrote the story on a scroll
and hid it in a loaf of bread.
"Take this to them, Zak,"
he said.

"What about the soldiers?" asked Zak.
"We know a way," said Anna.
"We could use the water channels."
"Good idea!" said Zak.

Zak, Anna, and Cyrus used a barrel
to float along the water channels.
They laughed and splashed each other.
Suddenly the barrel tipped.
They fell in the water and landed in
a filter station.

Roman soldiers pulled them from the water.

"What's this?" Stouticus said.

He grabbed the bread from Zak and took a bite
– right into the scroll!

Tacticus grabbed the scroll.

"A Christian!" he said to Zak.
"You're under arrest."
Anna ran back to the bakery.
"They captured Zak!" she cried.
"And Justin and Cyrus
followed them."
"What can we do?" said Ben.
Helena had an idea.
"Let's bake some special cakes
for Nero," she said.

Still following Zak, Justin and Cyrus
sailed right under Nero's palace.
They climbed through a grating
and hid behind a statue
in Nero's throne room.

They could see everything.
Nero was singing.
Tacticus dragged Zak in front of Nero.
"We captured this Christian in the waterway,"
he told Nero.

"What is he holding?"
demanded Nero.
"Some kind of story
about this Jesus,"
Tacticus replied.
"Read it, Christian,"
ordered Nero.

"No," replied Zak, "you only
want to make fun of Jesus.
I'd rather die than read it."

"Very well,"
Nero snapped.
"Soldier, you read it."
"Jesus and his disciples
were in a boat on a lake,"
Tacticus began.

Jesus was asleep in the stern.
Suddenly a terrible storm came up.
The waves poured over the side of the boat.
The disciples were terrified.

"Master, please wake up!" they shouted
at Jesus. "Don't you care if we drown?"
"Silence! Be still!" Jesus ordered.
As he spoke, the wind and the waves died down.
The sea was calm again.

"What kind of man is he?" the disciples asked. "Even the wind and the sea obey him."

"What a stupid story!" exclaimed Nero. "Throw this boy to the lions."

Justin and Cyrus saw it all. "I hope Ben gets here soon," Justin whispered.

Four strange figures came to the palace.
They were dressed as bakers from Gaul.
They pretended to speak like French people.
"We have brought a cake for the emperor," they said.
"And a poison cake for the prisoner."

Nero was delighted.
He handed the cake to Zak.
Zak realized who the baker
was. So he bit the cake.
He fell to the floor and
pretended he was dead.

Ben and Helena put Zak on the cart.
They started to take him away.
Then Zak sneezed.
Nero was furious.
"Stop them!" he ordered.
They were trapped.
"Ben! Over here!" whispered Justin.
Justin and Cyrus pushed over the statue.
Crash! It fell on the cart.
Flour filled the room.

Ben and the gang jumped through
the grating under the statue.
Tacticus gave Zak the scroll.
"Hurry, before I change my mind,"
he said.
Zak jumped and landed
on Justin's barrel.
"After them!" shouted Nero.

The soldiers chased them.
Ben and the children held on tight.
They escaped through the water.

Ben threw the scroll.
Some friends below
caught it.

That night, thanks to
Ben and the children, the
Christians in North Rome
had their story after all.

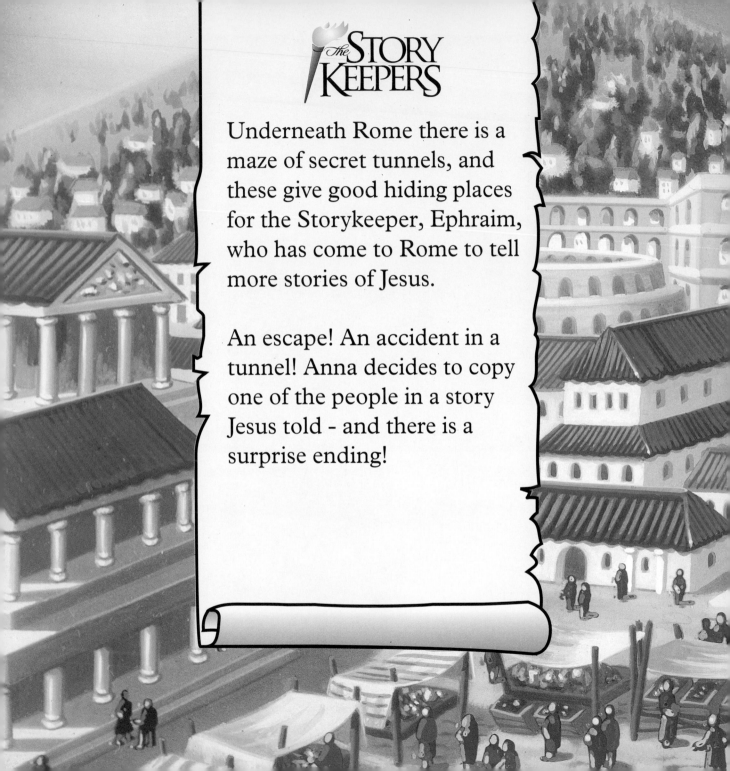

THE STORY KEEPERS

Underneath Rome there is a maze of secret tunnels, and these give good hiding places for the Storykeeper, Ephraim, who has come to Rome to tell more stories of Jesus.

An escape! An accident in a tunnel! Anna decides to copy one of the people in a story Jesus told - and there is a surprise ending!

THE STORY KEEPERS

Episode 3

Catacomb Rescue

Long ago, in the city of Rome,
there lived a mighty ruler.
His name was Nero.
He thought he was a god,
but the Christians knew he wasn't.
So Nero hated them.

One day there was a great fire.
Nero said the Christians started it,
and he sent his cruel soldiers after them.

Marcus, Justin, and Anna
lost their parents during the fire.
Ben the baker and his wife, Helena,
took them into their home.
There, in a time of great danger,
they told the children stories about Jesus.

This book is about the adventures
of the Storykeepers.

The STORY KEEPERS

Ben, Helena and the children were sneaking through the streets of Rome.

"Careful, everyone," Ben warned.
"We don't want to be seen.
Tonight you will meet Ephraim,
who was once with Jesus.
The soldiers would love to capture him."
Finally the group reached the secret meeting place.

"Ephraim!" Ben greeted his old friend.
"We are eager to hear your story!"
Ephraim laughed. "All right," he said.
And he began to tell this story.

One day a lawyer asked Jesus, "How should I live?" Jesus told this story. A Jew was traveling down a road. Some men robbed him and beat him up. They left him to die.

A temple priest saw the man.
But he did not stop to help.
Another man from the temple did not stop either.
But a Samaritan felt sorry for him.
He stopped and put the man on his own donkey.

The Samaritan took him to an inn and looked after him. The innkeeper was surprised.
"Usually Samaritans and Jews do not speak to each other," he said, "but this Samaritan helped a Jew."

Jesus asked the lawyer: "Which of these people showed us how to live?"
The lawyer answered, "The one who was kind to him."
"Do the same," said Jesus.

Anna and Justin listened carefully
to the story.
One of Nero's spies heard the story.
He told Nero about Ephraim.
Nero was furious.
"Find this man!" he ordered. "Search
every house in Rome. Close the gates.
No one may leave the city."

The next day Justin burst into the bakery.
"The soldiers are coming!" he cried.
"We've got to hide Ephraim!"
"Justin and Anna," said Ben, "take Ephraim
to the catacombs. Wait for me there.
And take these papers. They will help Ephraim
get out of the city."

After the soldiers had gone,
Ben made his way to the catacombs.
It was dark. He thought no one saw him.

But two soldiers,
Tacticus and Nihilus,
were following him.
They watched him
go in.

Ben found Ephraim and the children.
They hurried through the tunnels
of the catacombs.

Suddenly Ben heard a noise.
He turned and saw two shadows.
"We're being followed! Run!" he called.

"You go on with the children, Ben,"
said Ephraim. "It's me they're after."
"I'll carry you, old friend," said Ben.
But the soldiers were catching up.
"I have an idea," said Anna.
She kicked the wall of
the catacomb.

Rocks began to fall. Then the roof fell in.
But a wall of rocks separated Ben and Ephraim
from the children.
"I know another way out," said Anna.
"Go ahead without us."

Justin and Anna heard a voice behind them in the tunnel.

"Nihilus! Help me!" Tacticus called.

He had fallen into a pit.
But Nihilus ran away.
"Help yourself!" he shouted back.

"It's one of the soldiers.
He's trapped," said Justin.

Anna was frightened.

"What should we do?" she asked.

"Leave him," said Justin.

"Nihilus, help me please!" called the soldier.

"It's not right to leave him," said Anna.

"But he was going to arrest us," said Justin.

Anna felt sorry for
the soldier.
She grabbed his whip
to pull him out.
But she could not
hold on. She slipped.
Justin grabbed and
pulled.

Together the children pulled him out.
But they dropped Ephraim's papers.

Tacticus groaned.
"Are you all right?" asked Anna.
Tacticus rubbed the dirt
from his eyes.
He stared at
the children.

"You? You saved me?" he cried.
"But you are Christians.
I came in here to arrest you.
Why would you help me?"

"We were just doing what the Samaritan did," said Anna.
"What Samaritan?" Tacticus asked.
"In the story Ephraim told," Anna said.
"Take me to Ephraim," said Tacticus.

Outside the catacombs,
a crowd of people had gathered.
"We must go and fight the soldiers,"
someone said.
Ephraim was calming them down.
"We must learn to forgive," he said.
He told them another story Jesus told.

There was a servant who owed his king
a lot of money.
He could not pay it back.
"You must sell all you have," said the king.
"Give me time, I'll pay," said the man.
The king felt sorry for the servant.
He forgave him and let him go.

Then the servant met a friend who owed him money.
"Pay me what you owe!" he cried.
"I need more time!" the friend begged.
But the servant had him thrown into prison.

When the king heard about this he was angry.
"I let you off," he said, "but you did not do the same for your friend."
And he threw the man into prison.

"We must forgive those who hurt us," Ephraim concluded.
Just then Tacticus stepped forward.
"Are you Ephraim, the Christian storykeeper?" he asked.
"Did you tell these children the story of the Samaritan?
Another soldier left me to die, but because of your story
these children saved my life."

Tacticus
became
friends with
all the Christians
from that day.
"I will help you all I
can," he told Ben.
"I will make sure that Ephraim gets out
of Rome safely."

And Tacticus kept his word.

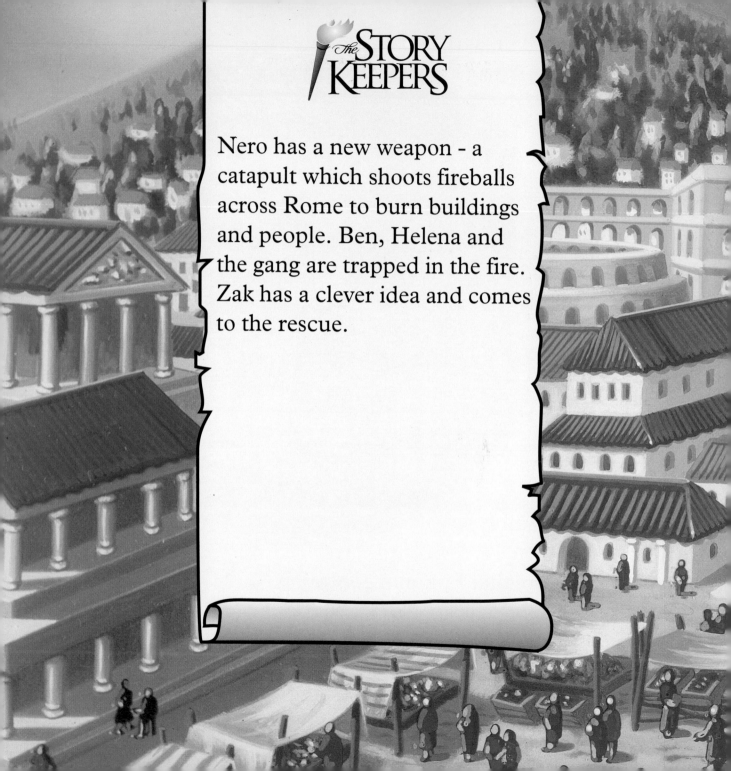

THE STORY KEEPERS

Nero has a new weapon - a catapult which shoots fireballs across Rome to burn buildings and people. Ben, Helena and the gang are trapped in the fire. Zak has a clever idea and comes to the rescue.

THE STORY KEEPERS

Episode 4

Ready, Aim, Fire!

Long ago, in the city of Rome,
there lived a mighty ruler.
His name was Nero.
He thought he was a god,
but the Christians knew he wasn't.
So Nero hated them.

One day there was a great fire.
Nero said the Christians started it,
and he sent his cruel soldiers after them.

Marcus, Justin, and Anna
lost their parents during the fire.
Ben the baker and his wife, Helena,
took them into their home.
There, in a time of great danger,
they told the children stories about Jesus.

This book is about the adventures
of the Storykeepers.

"Cyrus, can you see the messenger yet?" asked Zak.
He was worried. He was waiting for his famous uncle,
Mordecai.

Cyrus and Anna were hiding in a tree.
They were on the lookout.
"Not a sign," replied Cyrus.
"Keep looking. But stay under cover."

Suddenly Anna spotted a
man. He was being chased
by soldiers.
"Here he comes!" she called.
"Nihilus is going to catch
him!" Cyrus cried.
"I know what to do," Zak
said.

Zak put an arrow in his bow and
aimed at some barrels on a cart.
He fired, but he missed.
Ben grabbed a bow and fired.
Bull's-eye! Oil spilled out of
the barrels. The soldiers slipped
and slid.
And Mordecai disappeared into
the crowd.

Nihilus shook his fist.
"I will get you Christians!" he
shouted. "You can't hide from me
forever!"

Back at the safe house, Ben and the children
greeted Mordecai. The children were excited to
see Zak's uncle because he was a famous soldier.
"Tell us about your adventures!" they said.
Zak pushed them away.
"He does not have time to tell stories," said Zak.
But Mordecai loved children. He told them a story
about Jesus and some children.

One day parents brought their children to Jesus
to be blessed.
But the disciples told them to go away.

Jesus said, "Let the boys and girls come to me. My kingdom belongs to people who are like them." No wonder the children all loved Jesus!

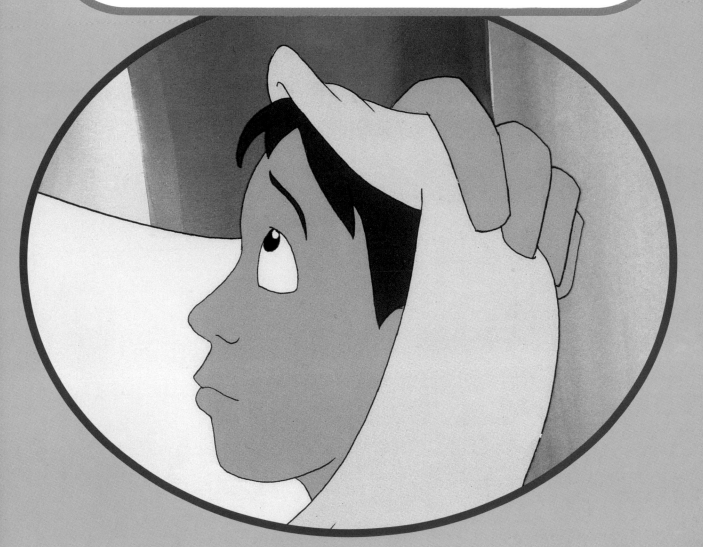

Zak was still unhappy.
He was ashamed that his
arrow had missed.
Ben said nothing. Nor did
Mordecai.
"I have something for
you, Zak," Mordecai said.
"It's a star of David from
your father."
Now Zak felt very proud.

At the palace, Nihilus reported back to Nero. He was still angry with the Christians.

"Let me destroy their houses, Caesar," he said. "I have a secret weapon that will shoot balls of fire at their homes."

Another soldier named Tacticus was a friend of Ben. He was worried when he heard about the plan. He told his servant, Darius, "We must warn Ben. He has a meeting tonight. Tell him that he is in danger."
Darius ran to find Ben.

At the meeting Ben told the Christians this story to make them brave:

Jesus and his disciples were going through the city of Jericho.
A blind man named Bartimaeus sat by the roadside calling out: "Son of David! Jesus! Help me!"

"Shh! Be quiet! Sit down!" The crowds shouted. But Jesus called the man to him.
"What do you want me to do for you?" he asked Bartimaeus.
"I want to see again," the man replied.

Jesus just looked at him, and Bartimaeus was able to see again. "Go home," said Jesus. "Your faith has made you see."

Darius burst into the room.
"There's going to be a fire!
The soldiers have a new weapon.
It shoots balls of flame!"
Suddenly a huge ball of fire dropped
from the sky. The house was set
alight.
Quickly, the gang put out
the flames.

"Tacticus will try to stop the bombing," said Darius.
"We cannot wait. We must escape," said Ben.
"Quickly, into the barrels," he ordered.
They did as Ben said. Justin and Darius rolled the barrels into a stream.
The Christians floated away past the soldiers.

Ben put Helena, Mordecai, Marcus, and Anna onto a wagon.

"Justin and I will take my baker's wagon, Zak," he said. "We'll meet you at the bakery."

Marcus and Anna were scared
by the fires.
"Why does Nero want to hurt us?"
they asked. "What have we done
wrong?"
Helena told them this story:

One day Jesus was in the synagogue,
the Jewish meeting house.
It was Sabbath, the day Jews are supposed
to do no work.

A man with a paralyzed hand was there.
The people watched Jesus. Would Jesus heal the man on the Sabbath?
"What is the right thing to do on the Sabbath?" Jesus asked. "To make someone better or let him die?"

"Stretch out your hand," Jesus said to the man.
And Jesus healed him.

Helena looked at the children.
"Sometimes you have to do what is right even if it gets you into trouble," she said.

Suddenly their horse reared in fright.
She bolted past Ben and Justin's wagon.
Zak couldn't control her. They were
heading directly into the fires!

Ben and Justin raced after them.
They caught up to the wagon.
"Jump!" called Ben to Helena.
She and the children jumped to safety
just in time.

But fires still blocked
their way.
"We're trapped!"
Justin cried.

"I have an idea," Zak said. "Cyrus, climb that statue and tie this rope on it. We'll fire the statue and knock a hole in the waterway."

Wham! Bull's-eye!
Water poured out
of the wall.

"You
did it, Zak,
you did it!"
Cyrus cried.
"Good shot!"
Mordecai said. "Your
father would be proud, Zak."

Thanks to Zak's idea, the fires were put out.
And all of the gang escaped.

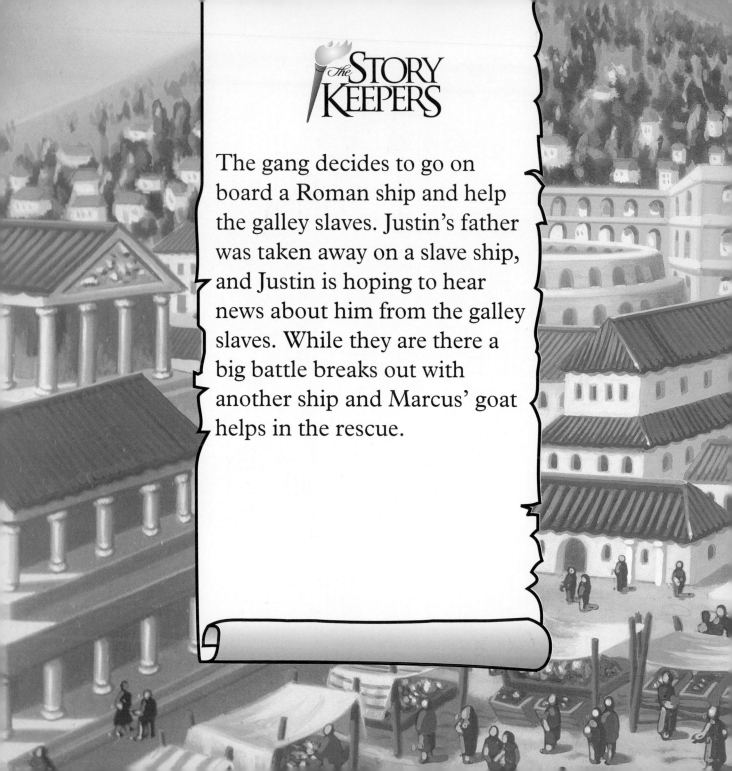

THE STORY KEEPERS

The gang decides to go on board a Roman ship and help the galley slaves. Justin's father was taken away on a slave ship, and Justin is hoping to hear news about him from the galley slaves. While they are there a big battle breaks out with another ship and Marcus' goat helps in the rescue.

The STORY KEEPERS

Episode 5

Sink or Swim

Long ago, in the city of Rome,
there lived a mighty ruler.
His name was Nero.
He thought he was a god,
but the Christians knew he wasn't.
So Nero hated them.

One day there was a great fire.
Nero said the Christians started it,
and he sent his cruel soldiers after them.

Marcus, Justin, and Anna
lost their parents during the fire.
Ben the baker and his wife, Helena,
took them into their home.
There, in a time of great danger,
they told the children stories about Jesus.

This book is about the adventures
of the Storykeepers.

The STORY KEEPERS

It was a dark, stormy night in
the city of Rome.
In the bakery Cyrus and Anna
were juggling rolls.
"I can't do six," said Anna.
"Yes, you can!" Cyrus replied. "Here!"
He tossed her six rolls hot from the oven.
"Ow!" Anna said, juggling faster and faster.
"I knew you could do it!" Cyrus laughed.

A knock sounded at the door.
"Who can that be?" said Helena.
Ben opened the door. A man lay
on the doorstep.
"Ben," the man groaned.
"Titus!" said Ben. He picked up
the man and carried him to bed.

Later, Titus told them what had happened.
"Because I am a Christian, the Roman soldiers sent me to a slave ship," he said. "It was terrible. The captain was cruel, and we hardly had any food. I escaped when we came ashore."

"My father was on a slave ship, too.
Do you know him?" asked Justin.
"There are many ships and hundreds
of slaves," Titus replied.
"How can we help them, Ben?"
asked Justin.
"We'll take our show to the ship!"
answered Ben.

The next day, Ben and the gang set up their show on the deck. The soldiers and sailors watched Anna and Cyrus juggle.

Justin and Ben hid in the lower part of the ship. Zak passed food to them through a porthole.

Justin took loaves to
the slaves down below.
"What are you doing here,
boy?" a slave named Andrew
asked.
"I'm looking for my father,"
Justin replied.

"The only thing you'll find
here is trouble," Andrew said.
"Now go, before you get us all
killed."

Suddenly a guard shouted:
"All slaves to the oars!
The captain has ordered
us to sea."
Ben, Helena, Zak, and
the children scrambled to
leave the ship.
Too late! They were
trapped on board, far from
shore.

A sailor led them to the captain's
cabin. He locked the door.
The ship began to roll. The children
were frightened. They had never
been to sea before.
So Ben told them a story Jesus told.

The rains fell.
The floods came.
The winds blew.
The houses rocked, just as this ship is doing right now.
The house built on the rock stood firm.
But the other house came down with a crash.

Suddenly the door burst open.
Hadrian the Fearless, the captain, stood in
the doorway.
"So these are the stowaways!" said Hadrian.
"They will work like everyone else."

"Take this mop," the captain said to Zak.

"You, give water to the soldiers," he ordered Justin.

"And you two stay here and clean," he said to Marcus and Cyrus.

"I'm a baker," said Ben.

"Excellent!" Hadrian said. "Go to the galley at once!"

The mate took Ben, Helena, and Anna to the kitchen.

The cook was preparing soup for the slaves. It looked awful.

"I'm supposed to help with the bread," said Ben.

"Good. I could use some help," said the cook.

Soon, the smell of
warm baked bread
filled the kitchen.
"Mmm. What is
that?" the cook asked.
"Our special bread.
Here, taste some,"
Helena offered.
While the cook gobbled the
bread, Ben made fresh good
soup for the prisoners.

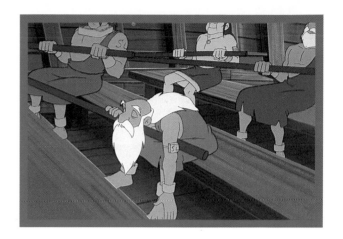

Meanwhile, Justin took water to the guards.
One of the slaves begged him for a sip.
But the guard dragged Justin away.
"He's dying of thirst," said Justin. "I'll
take his place."
The guard laughed. "This I've got
to see! Go ahead, little man!"
he scoffed.
So Justin took the man's
place and began
to row.

Ben and Helena took the soup to the slaves.
As they ate Ben told them a story.

One day Jesus was teaching people about God's way. The house was packed.

Four people were carrying a friend who couldn't walk. They could not get in.

The four carried their friend on to the roof. They lowered him through the roof to the feet of Jesus.
When Jesus saw how they trusted him, hc said to their friend: "Get up, pick up your mat, and walk."

The man got up and began to walk. Everyone was amazed. "We've never seen anything like this!" they said.

The slaves, too, were amazed. They enjoyed the story nearly as much as the soup.

Suddenly, there was a crash.
"We're under attack!" shouted a slave.
"Prepare to be boarded!"
A ship had smashed into the hull.
Water poured into the hold.
Ben and the gang clambered into the soup pot
and floated in the water.

As the pot passed the ship some slaves called out: "Help us! We're drowning!"
The gang clambered back on board.
"They're still chained," said Justin.

"I saw some keys in the captain's cabin," said Cyrus. Thastus, Marcus's pet goat, butted the door.
The door burst open, and Cyrus found the keys.

Ben helped Helena, Marcus, and Anna
to escape to another ship. He and Justin
took the keys to the slave hold.
By now many of the slaves were waist
deep in water.

Justin took several deep breaths and dived. Could he unlock the slaves in time?

"Hurry. We can't last much longer," they cried.

Just in time, Justin turned the key and set them free.

One slave, Andrew, was left.

The ship was sinking. Justin and Andrew
were still on board.
When all seemed lost, Justin and Andrew
burst from the water.
Thanks to the bravery of Justin, all the
slaves were rescued. Ben and the gang were
picked up by a rebel ship. And everyone
arrived home, safe and sound.

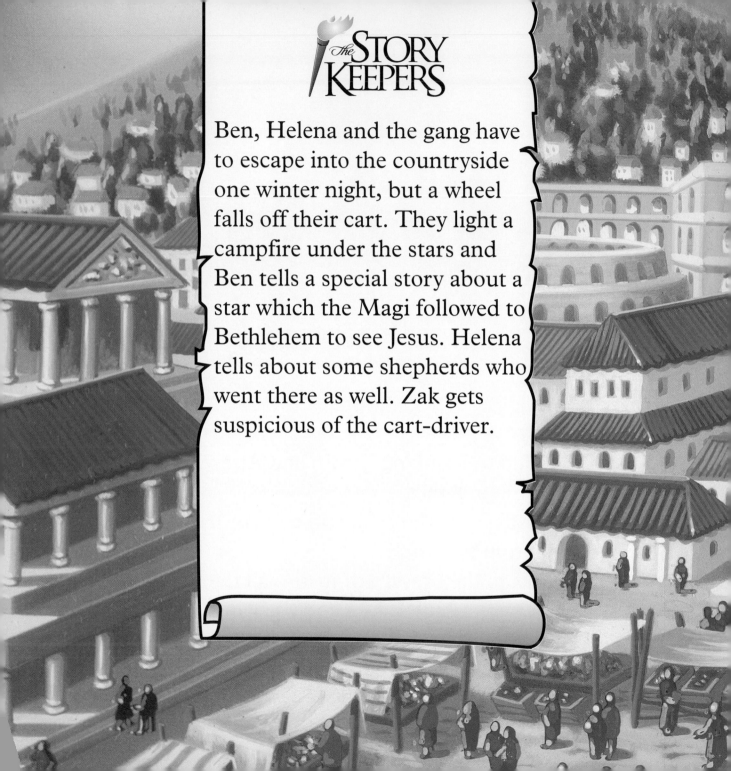

THE STORY KEEPERS

Ben, Helena and the gang have to escape into the countryside one winter night, but a wheel falls off their cart. They light a campfire under the stars and Ben tells a special story about a star which the Magi followed to Bethlehem to see Jesus. Helena tells about some shepherds who went there as well. Zak gets suspicious of the cart-driver.

THE STORY KEEPERS

Episode 6

Starlight Escape

L ong ago, in the city of Rome, there lived a mighty ruler. His name was Nero. He thought he was a god, but the Christians knew he wasn't. So Nero hated them.

One day there was a great fire. Nero said the Christians started it, and he sent his cruel soldiers after them.

Marcus, Justin, and Anna lost their parents during the fire. Ben the baker and his wife, Helena, took them into their home. There, in a time of great danger, they told the children stories about Jesus.

This book is about the adventures of the Storykeepers.

The sky was clear and bright.
An old man named Milo was taking
Ben and the gang to a secret meeting
in the town of Ostia.
Zak was worried. What if the guards
saw them?

Suddenly, horsemen appeared and began to chase them.

"Hold on, everyone!" Milo cried. He cracked his whip and the horses took off running.

"Are you trying to get us killed?" Zak yelled.

Milo veered to the left. The guards went to the right.
"Lost them!" said Milo.
But they had broken a wheel.
"We'll never get to Ostia now," Zak said.

While Milo fixed the wheel,
Helena told the children a story.

The story begins in the small town of Nazareth. Joseph and Mary lived there. They were engaged to be married.

One day Mary had a message from God.
"God is pleased with you. You will have a son
and will call him Jesus. He will be great and will
be called the Son of God."

"I will do whatever God wants," Mary said. "Let it happen to me as you have said."

The sky was full of angels singing, "Glory to God in heaven, and peace to all people on earth."
The shepherds went to see Jesus and worshiped him.

"Do you know why I like the story of Jesus' birth?" Helena asked. "Because ordinary shepherds were the first to see Jesus."

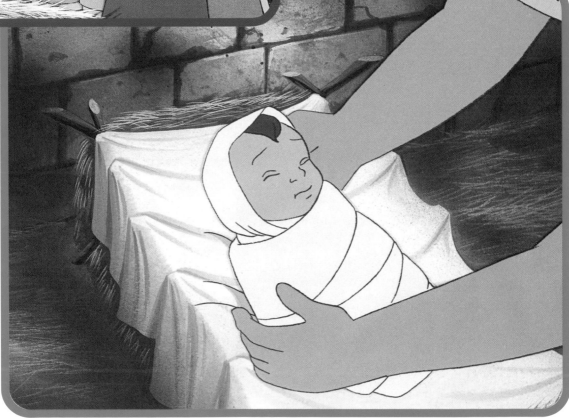

"I'll go and see why Milo is taking so long,"
said Zak.
He asked Milo a question, but Milo didn't answer.
"This old coot can't hear a thing," Zak scoffed.
"Watch it, sonny," Milo said. "It's a long walk to
Ostia."
Zak blushed.

Soon they were back in the wagon, rattling down
a rough riverbed.

"Whoever heard of driving down a riverbed?"
Zak grumbled.

"Well, one thing's for sure," said Ben. "Nero's
guards will never spot us down here."

At last they stopped
outside a dark inn.
"I'll be right back,"
said Milo.
Zak stopped him.
"Wait! Where are you going?"
"To find out where your meeting is," Milo snapped.

"I don't trust him," Zak grumbled to Ben.
"Calm down," Ben said. "Milo knows what he is doing."

Ben and the children waited,
shivering in the dark.
Suddenly they saw a shooting
star in the sky. So Ben told
the children another story
about some men who
followed a very special star
to Jerusalem.

"They knew that the star meant a king had been born," said Ben. "So they went to the palace of King Herod, a wicked man."

"We have come to worship the child who was born to be king of the Jews," they said to King Herod. "Do you know where we may find him?" Herod was worried. He didn't want someone else to be king.

King Herod sent the visitors to Bethlehem.
"When you find him, come back and tell me where he is," he said.

They found the house where the child was. He was staying there with his parents, Mary and Joseph.

They gave him gifts.
Gold fit for a king, sweet-smelling
incense, and myrrh.

Not long after, the magi left for their own country. They did not go back to Herod. The king was angry, and he was determined to get rid of the child.

"Search the city of Bethlehem. Kill every boy under the age of two," he ordered his soldiers.

That very night an angel appeared to Joseph in a dream and warned him. He, Mary, and Jesus escaped to Egypt.

"King Herod sounds even worse than Emperor Nero!" said Cyrus.
"I like those stories," said Marcus.
"So do I," said a deep voice behind them.
Everyone jumped with fright.
It was a Roman soldier!

Ben recognized the big man. "This is an old friend," he said. "Yes, he's a Roman guard. But he is a Christian too."

Everyone thanked Milo for his help.
Then Zak said, "I'm sorry, Milo, for not
trusting you."
Milo replied, "Ah, you were just looking out
for your friends."
"Yes, but I went too far," Zak admitted.
"A trip like that makes everyone jittery," Milo
said. "Why, a long time ago I took a young
couple to Egypt. They were called Joseph
and Mary, and they had a baby called Jesus.
I wonder what happened to them?"

Milo went off, still talking with himself.
And Zak stood watching as the horse and
wagon disappeared into the night.

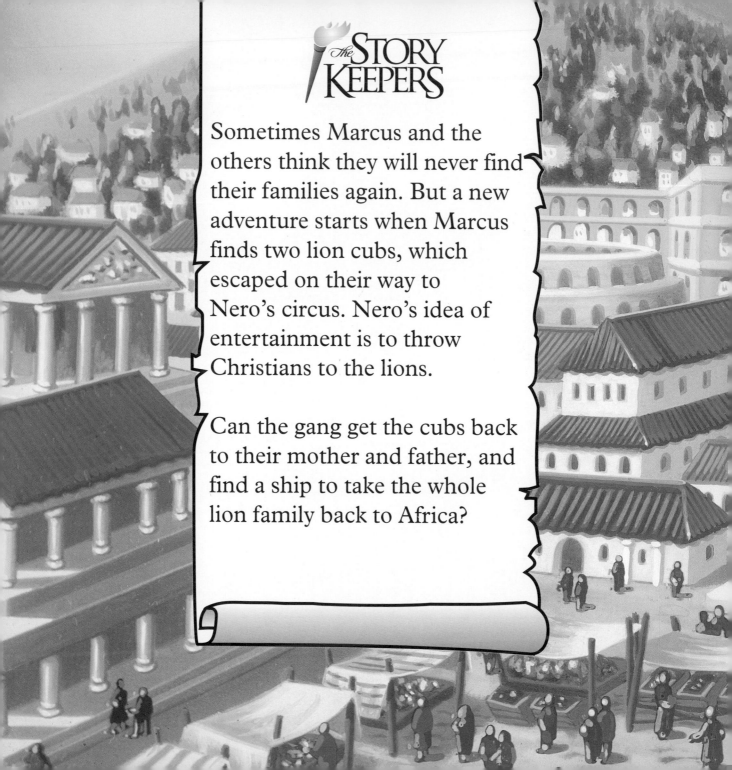

THE STORY KEEPERS

Sometimes Marcus and the others think they will never find their families again. But a new adventure starts when Marcus finds two lion cubs, which escaped on their way to Nero's circus. Nero's idea of entertainment is to throw Christians to the lions.

Can the gang get the cubs back to their mother and father, and find a ship to take the whole lion family back to Africa?

Episode 7

Roar in the Night

Long ago, in the city of Rome,
there lived a mighty ruler.
His name was Nero.
He thought he was a god,
but the Christians knew he wasn't.
So Nero hated them.

One day there was a great fire.
Nero said the Christians started it,
and he sent his cruel soldiers after them.

Marcus, Justin, and Anna
lost their parents during the fire.
Ben the baker and his wife, Helena,
took them into their home.
There, in a time of great danger,
they told the children stories about Jesus.

This book is about the adventures
of the Storykeepers.

It was a stormy night. Inside the bakery,
Ben and Helena were tucking the children
in bed.

"Justin, do you think it is raining where
mother and dad are?" asked Marcus.

"Don't worry," said Ben. "We'll find them
one day."

"We'll keep on looking for them," said Helena. "Just like the shepherd that Jesus told a story about."

A shepherd had a hundred sheep. He discovered one of them was missing.

He looked everywhere. Behind
trees. Under rocks. In the bushes.
He kept looking.

When he found the sheep he was so happy. He carried the sheep back to his farm on his shoulders.

His friends were happy for him. They had a wonderful party because he had found his sheep.

Next day, Marcus wanted to play "find the lost sheep." "I'm helping Ben," said Justin. "We are making icing," said Anna. So Marcus played with Thastus, the goat.

Marcus heard a noise.
"Aachoo!"
He looked around
and saw two lion
cubs in the hay.
They had escaped
from a ship in the port.
But Marcus did not
know this.

Marcus thought the cubs were kittens. He gave them milk. They played with the hens and the other animals. What a noise they made! Helena came to see what was going on.
"I was only playing hide and seek with my kittens," Marcus told Helena.

"Can we keep them, please?" Marcus
asked Ben and Helena.
"Just for a while," said Ben.
Marcus was pleased. "I'll look after you,"
he told the cubs.
Zak was angry. He knew that the kittens
were lion cubs. Grown-up lions ate
Christians in the arena.

Ben went to see his friend
Amicus, who owned a circus.
"Have you lost two lion
cubs?" Justin asked him.
"They belong to the Emperor
Nero," replied Amicus. He
had an idea. He sent Ben to
Saleem, the captain of a ship
in the port.

Saleem and his family were Christians.
Ben asked Saleem to take the cubs back to
their home in Africa.
But Ben had no money to pay Saleem.
So Ben told a story instead.

Everywhere Jesus went crowds came to see him. Children, people who could not walk, sick people. They all wanted to touch him.

One day, some people brought a man who could not hear or speak.

Jesus took the man away by himself. He put his finger in his ears, spat, and touched his tongue. Jesus looked up and said: "Be opened!"

The man began to speak. And he could hear! Jesus told the man and his friends not to tell anyone.

"But I am going to tell everyone this story when I get back home in Africa," said Saleem.

Ben told Marcus that Saleem would
take the cubs.
"They will be safe in Africa," said
Ben.
Marcus was sad. But he knew it was
for the best. "I'm going to miss you,"
he said to the cubs.

Meanwhile, the lion trainer was angry. "Find those cubs!" he ordered his men. They took a pack of dogs and searched from house to house until they reached the bakery.

There was a knock on the door.
"It's Amicus. I'll open the door,"
said Ben.
The gang was shocked – it was the
lion trainer!
The men and the dogs rushed into
the bakery. They seized the cubs
and took them off in a cart.

"We've got to rescue them," said Marcus.
"They have their mother as well," said Amicus.
"We must save her too."
"We will need your cage and wagon," said Ben.

Ben, Amicus, Zak, and the children drove
in secret to the lion trainer's camp.
The children found a giant elephant horn
in Amicus's wagon. They set it up on the
hill above the training camp. Zak blew it by
mistake! It frightened an
elephant in the camp. The
elephant bellowed and
pulled at his chain.

All the guards rushed to see what was happening.

The lion cages were left unguarded. Amicus crept to the cages and opened the doors.

"Leo. Theo!" called Marcus to the two lion cubs.

"Call for your mother!"
said Marcus to the
cubs.
"Meow!"
"Meow!" The mother
lion heard the cries.
She leapt from her
cage on to the wagon.
Amicus drove off as
fast as he could.

Down the bumpy road to the dockside
went the wagon. Dogs and more guards
chased after them.

"Here they come," Captain Saleem
shouted to his men. "Prepare to cast off!"

It was too late. Before they could get the lions and their cages on board, the guards arrived.

"Take them!" the trainer ordered. He knocked Amicus to the ground.

Ben and Helena stopped to help their
friend. They thought that they would be
captured. But suddenly Mangler, Amicus's
oldest lion, saw them. He roared.
"Man eater!" the guards shouted. They
all ran away.
Amicus laughed. Mangler was his friend.

Amicus put his arms
around Mangler's neck.
"Good work, Mangler,
my old friend!" he said.
The sailors lifted the
cages on board.

"Good-bye," said Marcus to the cubs.
"You found your family after all. Maybe
someday I'll find my parents too."

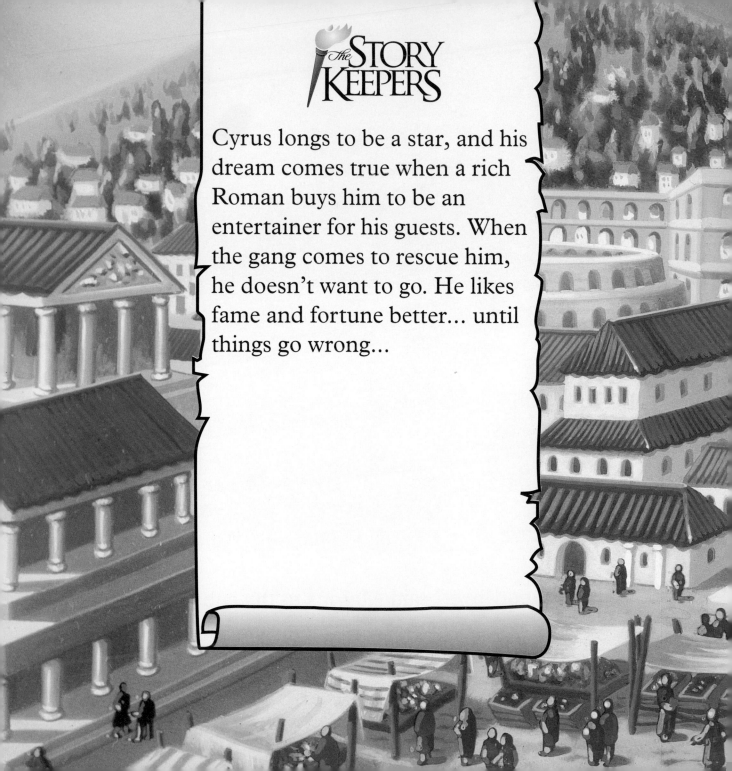

THE STORY KEEPERS

Cyrus longs to be a star, and his dream comes true when a rich Roman buys him to be an entertainer for his guests. When the gang comes to rescue him, he doesn't want to go. He likes fame and fortune better... until things go wrong...

THE STORY KEEPERS

Episode 8

Captured!

Long ago, in the city of Rome,
there lived a mighty ruler.
His name was Nero.
He thought he was a god,
but the Christians knew he wasn't.
So Nero hated them.

One day there was a great fire.
Nero said the Christians started it,
and he sent his cruel soldiers after them.

Marcus, Justin, and Anna
lost their parents during the fire.
Ben the baker and his wife, Helena,
took them into their home.
There, in a time of great danger,
they told the children stories about Jesus.

This book is about the adventures
of the Storykeepers.

The STORY KEEPERS

Cyrus was showing off again.
He was balancing lamps on top of one another.
"This reminds me of the shows I used to give with my parents," he said.
"I'm a record breaker."
Justin did not like Cyrus's boasting.

Suddenly the door burst open.
A squad of soldiers broke into the room.
"Run!" shouted Ben to the children.
Cyrus, Anna, and Marcus ran to the
square.
"We're not going to make it," Anna cried.
"Hide! I'll take care of them," Cyrus
shouted.

Cyrus jumped onto the canopy of a shop.
The soldiers ran up to him. They threw their spears.
Cyrus dodged and dropped onto a cart below.

Barrels of honey and bales of hay flew into the air,
splattering the soldiers with hay and honey.
Anna and Marcus laughed. Cyrus ran away, but bumped
into a carriage in the road. Before he could move,
he was arrested by Lucian, a soldier.

"Bravo, my boy! Encore!" said the man in the carriage. His name was Flavian. He was a rich man and had lots of slaves.

"That boy is just what I need,"
said Flavian. He gave Lucian a bag of
money. Then he handed Cyrus to
Zeto, the man in charge of his slaves.
He was cruel and frightened Cyrus.
Anna and Marcus saw it all.

When they arrived at the rich man's palace, Cyrus turned to run away.

"Come back here!" shouted Zeto. But Cyrus laughed. He swung on a beam across a pond. The beam snapped. Cyrus splashed into the water.

Flavian watched and laughed.
"Isn't he wonderful?" the rich man said to his friends.
"I'd better get home to my family," said Cyrus.
"Nonsense! You're going to be a star here!" replied Flavian.

Flavian dressed Cyrus in fine
clothes. He gave him the finest
fruits and food. Cyrus received a
new name, "Cyroo, Prince of
Jugglers," and his own stage.
Cyrus was a star.
But this only made the other slaves more angry.

Anna told Ben the news about Cyrus and Flavian.
"He saved Marcus and me from the soldiers!" she said.
Justin was not so sure. "If he hadn't been such a
show-off he would not have got captured," he said.
"Justin, Cyrus is still part of this family. You should treat
him like a brother," said Ben.

To explain, Helena told a story that Jesus told about a farmer who had two sons.

The younger son came one day to his father. "Give me my share of the farm," he demanded. The farmer divided everything between them. The next day the younger son left to see the world. He wasted his money. He lost everything.

Then the harvest failed all over the land.
There he was, no money, no friends, and no food.
He found a job with a farmer, feeding pigs.
He was so hungry he even ate the pigs' food.

Zak interrupted. "Come on! We need to rescue Cyrus!"

"What about the story?" Marcus asked.

"Helena will finish the story later," said Ben.

Ben, Anna, Justin, and Zak rode to Flavian's palace in Ben's cart.

Anna and Justin waited until the guards had passed. They looked inside and were amazed. Cyrus was lying on a fine bed in a beautiful room.

"Cyrus! Over here," whispered Anna.
"We're here to help you escape," added Justin.

"I want to stay," replied Cyrus.
"I'm going to be famous here."
Justin and Anna were surprised.
"What about Ben and Helena?"
said Anna. "They love you!"
It was no good. Cyrus still said,
"No, thanks."

Cyrus was so proud of himself. Now he was Flavian's star entertainer. Flavian showed him off to his friends. "Here is Cyroo, Prince of Jugglers!" he announced.

One night while Cyrus was asleep everything changed. A shout woke him up.

"Slave revolt!"
Cyrus saw a group of slaves chasing
Flavian's guards. He smelled smoke.
The slaves had set fire to the palace!

The next day Cyrus found the rich
slave owner wandering in the garden.
"Look at this place. I'm ruined,"
Flavian cried.

Cyrus tried to help. But
Flavian blamed Cyrus.
He pulled his sword to
attack Cyrus.
Cyrus ran for his life.

Back in the bakery Helena finished telling the story about the two brothers.

The younger son was starving. "I know what. I'll go home. I'll say, 'Father, I've done wrong. I don't deserve to be called your son.'"

While he was still a long way off, his father saw him and ran to meet him. The farmer told his servants, "Quick, get his best clothes out. Get him a ring and sandals. We'll have a feast tonight."

The brother was out in the fields. He became angry and didn't want to come to the party.
His father said, "We had to celebrate. Your brother's back with us again."

As Helena finished the story they saw Cyrus standing outside.

Justin went to meet Cyrus.
Justin looked at his "brother" all alone in the
cold. He remembered the story of the farmer.
He went up to Cyrus and hugged him.
"Welcome home, Cyrus," Justin said.

It's Nero's birthday again, and his chief guard, Tacticus, refuses to bow down and worship him. Tacticus finally admits he is a Christian and is thrown into prison.

Ben and the gang disguise themselves in the Empress's clothes and veils to get into the palace. One of the Empress's servants, Miriam, helps them. Will Tacticus have to die?

Episode 9

Trapped!

L ong ago, in the city of Rome,
there lived a mighty ruler.
His name was Nero.
He thought he was a god,
but the Christians knew he wasn't.
So Nero hated them.

One day there was a great fire.
Nero said the Christians started it,
and he sent his cruel soldiers after them.

Marcus, Justin, and Anna
lost their parents during the fire.
Ben the baker and his wife, Helena,
took them into their home.
There, in a time of great danger,
they told the children stories about Jesus.

This book is about the adventures
of the Storykeepers.

Miriam was the Empress Poppaea's
servant. She was also a secret
Christian.
One morning she was helping Ben
and Helena bake a cake for Nero's
birthday.

There was a knock. It was a soldier. His name was Tacticus. "I cannot come to the meeting tonight. I have to meet the Emperor," said Tacticus. "He does not know I am a Christian. Only my best friends know," he said. Ben told Tacticus a story.

One day Jesus took his disciples to the top
of a mountain. A cloud covered them all.
Then an amazing thing happened.
Jesus' clothes became very bright.

His friends saw Jesus
talking to two men.
Suddenly, through the mist,
they heard a voice.
"This is my Son. You must
do what he says."
Then the two strangers
vanished.

The disciples were sure the voice was God's.

"Up until then," said Ben, "the disciples did not realize who Jesus was. Jesus told them not to tell anyone yet."
"I can understand how he felt," said Tacticus.

Later that day in the
palace, some workers put
a large statue of Nero's
head on an altar.
Nero was very pleased.
"Worship me!" he told
everyone.

"Hail Nero. Hail Nero!" cried Nihilus and his friends.

They sprinkled incense on a flame in front of the bust. Then they knelt down. But Tacticus did not move.

"Bow to me, Tacticus!" Nero commanded.

"I can't," replied Tacticus.

"You must bow down before me at my party tomorrow, or you will die," said Nero.

Meanwhile, Miriam and Anna were
in the Empress's bedroom. Miriam was
showing the Empress's clothes and perfume
to Anna. Suddenly, they heard a bang.
They peeped into the throne room and
heard Nero say, "Take Tacticus away."

Anna ran back to the bakery.
"Tacticus will be killed if he doesn't worship
Nero," Anna told Ben.
"Why couldn't Tacticus keep quiet about
being a Christian?" asked Cyrus.

"It was the same for Jesus," replied Ben. "He wanted to go to Jerusalem for the Great Feast. He could not keep hiding who he was. But he knew he had many enemies in the city who wanted to kill him."

Outside the city, in Bethany village, Jesus sent two of his disciples to find a donkey. "Bring it back with you," said Jesus.

Some people asked them, "What are you doing?"
"The Master, Jesus, needs it. We will send it back soon," the disciples replied.

Later that day, Jesus rode on the donkey into the city. People cheered him like a hero. Many thought he was God's chosen leader. Some people waved branches. Others threw branches and clothes on the road.

"It was very brave of Jesus to reveal who he really was when he had so many enemies," said Ben.
"But Tacticus must not," said Anna. "Nero will kill him."
"Don't worry," said Ben. "We'll break Tacticus out of the palace."

At dawn, Ben and Zak sailed down the aqueduct to the palace.

They sawed through iron bars and got inside.

Disguised as guards, they began to look for Tacticus's cell. But they bumped into some real guards.

"Where are your papers?" they demanded.

Then Ben and Zak heard
another voice. "There you are!
We've been looking everywhere
for you two." It was Miriam.
She gave them a pile of plates.
"The Empress is waiting for
these," she said.
The guards were frightened
of the Empress, so they let Ben
and Zak go.

"Now for Tacticus," said Ben.
They discovered their friend around
the corner. He was in chains.
Ben and Zak watched Nihilus drag
Tacticus before Nero.

All eyes turned to Tacticus. What gift would he give?

In his throne room Nero sat proudly. It was his birthday. "Bring forth Caesar's gifts!" shouted the chief courtier. "Our gift is a show," said a group of acrobats. "Mine is a golden bracelet," said another man.

Would Tacticus bow before the statue of Nero? "My gift is a story told long ago by a great man," said Tacticus.

He told a story about a man who planted a new vineyard. He rented it to some grape farmers.
After the harvest, he sent people to collect his share of the grapes.

The farmers beat them up because they were too greedy to share the harvest with the owner.
In the end, the man sent his son. And they killed him.
So the owner threw out the greedy farmers and put others in their place.

"Who was the great man who first told that story?" Nero asked.

"Jesus, the Christ, my lord," said Tacticus.

"How dare you! I am your god. Worship me!" roared Nero.

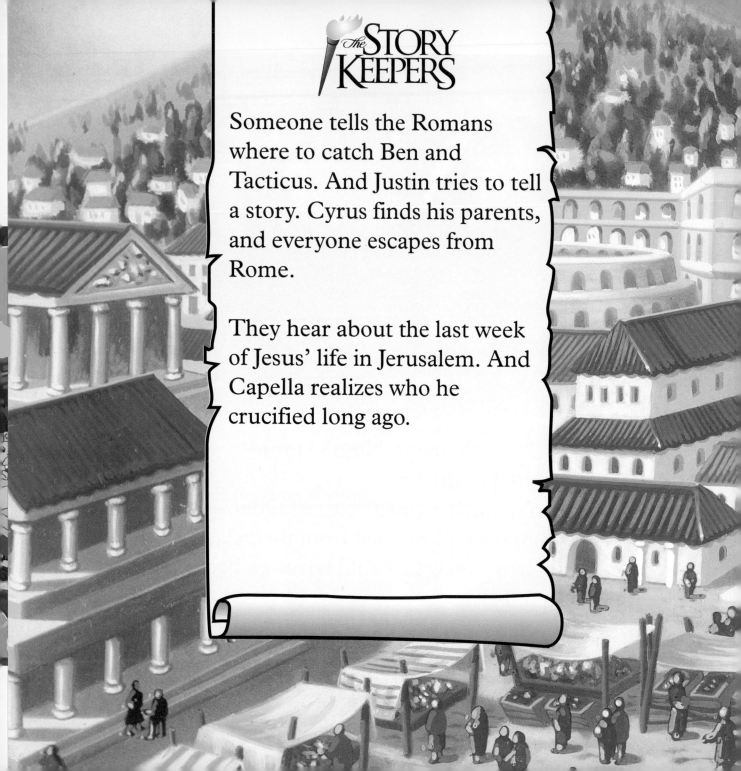

![The Story Keepers logo]

Someone tells the Romans where to catch Ben and Tacticus. And Justin tries to tell a story. Cyrus finds his parents, and everyone escapes from Rome.

They hear about the last week of Jesus' life in Jerusalem. And Capella realizes who he crucified long ago.

Long ago, in the city of Rome,
there lived a mighty ruler.
His name was Nero.
He thought he was a god,
but the Christians knew he wasn't.
So Nero hated them.

One day there was a great fire.
Nero said the Christians started it,
and he sent his cruel soldiers after them.

Marcus, Justin, Anna and Cyrus
lost their parents during the fire.
Ben the baker and his wife, Helena,
took them into their home.
There, in a time of great danger,
they told the children stories about Jesus.

This book is about the adventures
of the Storykeepers.

Nero's soldiers were
looking for Ben. Ben
was worried that
someone would betray
him.

Suddenly a friendly soldier named Darius arrived.
"Guards are looking in every house for Christians,"
he told Ben.

Ben decided that he must hide in the catacombs with
their friend Tacticus and some other Christians. When
he got there Ben told them a story about Jesus.

Jesus and his friends sat down for a special meal, called Passover. "One of you sitting having supper with me will hand me over to the religious leaders," said Jesus. This surprised Jesus' friends. They all said they would not.

"It is one of you," Jesus said again. Then he took some bread and said grace and broke the loaf in pieces. He gave it to his friends and said: "This is my very self, my body broken for you."

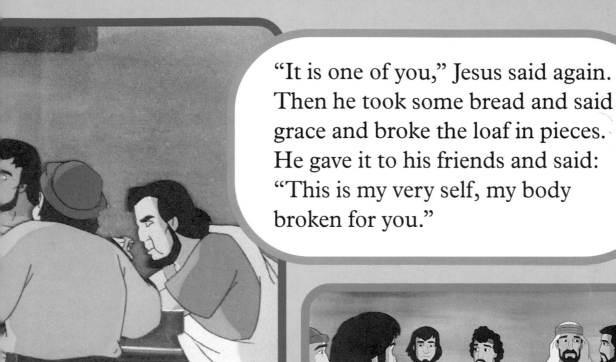

Then he took a cup of wine. He gave thanks to God and passed it to his friends.
"This is my very self, my blood. I will die. Then all people will know God loves everyone everywhere," said Jesus.

Meanwhile back at the bakery, there was a bang on the door. It was the wicked centurion Nihilus and his guards. Someone had betrayed Ben.

Zak ran to warn Ben. "The bakery is surrounded!" he exclaimed. "If you do not give yourself up Nihilus will burn down the bakery with Helena and the children in it."

Helena continued the
story Ben had been telling.

Jesus and his friends
were walking to a village.
Jesus told them, "You are all
going to run away. You are all
going to let me down."
"I'll never do such a
thing. I won't let you
down," replied Peter.
The other friends said
the same.

Jesus smiled and said: "Peter, before the cock crows twice, before dawn tomorrow, you will say three times that you do not even know me."

"I'll die for you first!" exclaimed Peter.

"Peter did not realize what he was saying,"
Helena went on. "What Jesus said would
come true."
Helena had no time to continue.
The guards outside were getting ready to
burn the bakery.

Nihilus stood outside the
bakery. "Board it up!
Burn it down!" he
ordered.
The guards obeyed and
began.
Inside the bakery Helena
and the children heard
the hammers banging.
They were really scared.

Suddenly Cyrus heard a sound
beneath their feet.
"Clang!"
"Everybody dig!"
Everyonc grabbed spoons, cups
and bowls and began to dig towards
the noise.
Just in time! The bakery was in flames.
They all disappeared into the tunnel
and made their way to a secret cavern
below the city.

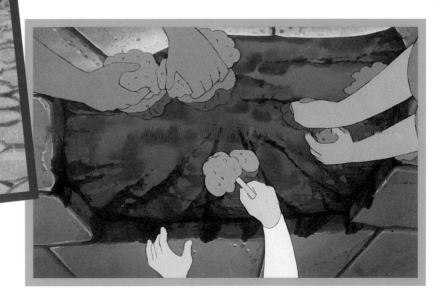

The guards searched for Ben for over a week. They found no sign of him.
But then one of the guards found a map. It pointed to the cavern where Ben was hiding.

Ben did not know he was in danger. So he told everyone a story about Jesus.

Jesus and his friends walked to a garden called Gethsemane. He asked them to sit and stay awake while he prayed.
Three times Jesus went away to pray. Three times he came back. But his friends could not stay awake.

Then Jesus heard noises. It was a group of guards from the temple in Jerusalem. With them was Judas, one of his friends.
Judas came towards Jesus. He kissed Jesus on the cheek. "Teacher," said Judas.

That was the signal for the guards. They seized Jesus and led him out of the garden. Jesus just let them do it.

Just as Ben finished, Roman soldiers burst into the cave.
"Nihilus wants him alive," one of them shouted.
The Christians knew what to do. They doused all the torches. In the darkness they all escaped through another passage, except for Marcus, Ben and Justin.
They were thrown into jail.

The two boys were scared.
So Ben told them a story
about Jesus' friend Peter.

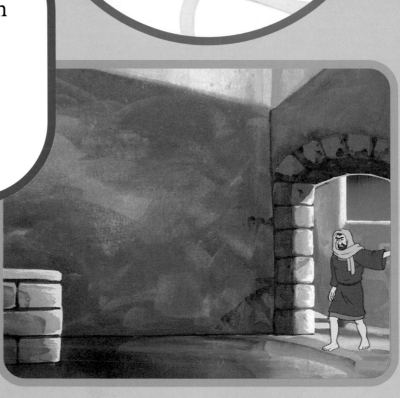

Peter was frightened
when Jesus was taken
away. He followed
behind. He did not
want anyone to see
him. So he waited
outside.

"You were with Jesus, that man from Nazareth." Peter turned. It was a servant girl who spoke. Peter said he was not. He said it three times. A cock crew. Peter remembered that Jesus had said that he would let him down.

Peter saw the guards take Jesus away. It made him very sad. They took Jesus to Pilate, the Roman governor.

People told lies about Jesus. They called him a rebel, a traitor and a troublemaker.
"Haven't you anything to say?" Pilate asked Jesus. "Why don't you answer them?"
Jesus still said nothing.

Before Ben could go on Nihilus stopped him and led Ben away. When they were on their own Justin continued the story instead of Ben.

At the feast the Romans used to set one prisoner free. Pilate wanted to release Jesus. But the crowd shouted: "Free Barabbas!"
Barabbas was a freedom fighter.

"What shall I do with the man you call the king?" Pilate asked the crowd. "Nail him to a cross!" the crowd replied, and shouted for Barabbas. Pilate let Barabbas go and ordered that Jesus be flogged.

Soldiers dressed Jesus in a red cloak.
They put a crown of thorns on his head.
"Hail, your majesty. Hail, king of the Jews,"
the soldiers jeered.
They took Jesus away to execute him.

Meanwhile Ben was in trouble. Nihilus had taken him before Nero. "Ask him if he is the leader of the Christians. Ask him about treason! Treachery! Sabotage!"

"Well, baker. Are you not the Christian leader?" demanded Nero.

"Yes, I am," repled Ben.

This made Nero furious. He leapt from his throne. "Take the baker away and kill him," he ordered.

Ben was put in jail with Justin and Marcus.
The head guard was called Capella. He mocked his
prisoners about Jesus.
"What do you know about Jesus?" asked Justin.
"I was there when he died," replied Capella. "A common
criminal."

In Jerusalem executions were held at a place called Skull Hill. Two terrorists were executed with him. On the top of the cross someone hung a sign: "King of the Jews." But he said, "Father forgive them. They don't know what they are doing."

Later, when Capella returned, Ben continued the story.

A man named Joseph from Arimathea went to the Roman governor, Pilate. He wanted permission to bury Jesus. Joseph and his friends carried Jesus' body to a tomb in a garden. The men rolled a huge stone over the entrance. Then they left.

Just as Ben was speaking there was a noise outside. It was Cyrus's parents and their circus friends. They were swinging across the roofs of the prison. This was so the guards would not see what was really happening.

While the sentries watched the acrobatics show,
Zak, Helena and Anna drove a large elephant
through the compound wall.
They broke into the stockade.
The prisoners escaped in a wagon. But Ben
would not leave.

"You should have escaped when you had the chance," said the guard.
"Then you would never have heard the rest of the story," replied Ben.
So Ben continued where he had left off.

The next day was Shabbat, the day we Jews cannot work. The day after that, some women friends of Jesus brought sweet oils to put on Jesus' body. They were surprised to find that the large stone had been rolled away.

"You won't find Jesus here. He has risen," a young man told them.

The women told Jesus' friends. Peter and John ran back to check. "It's just as they said!" John declared.

Mary was left alone crying.
"Why are you weeping?" a man asked her.
She tried to speak. But the man said her name: "Mary."
Mary looked up.
"Teacher!" she said.
"Don't hold on to me, Mary," he said.
Mary understood.

When Capella had heard the whole story, he refused to obey Nero's orders to kill Ben. Capella was attacked by the guards but the gang got Ben and Capella away. Capella was badly wounded. "At least I managed to hear the rest of the story," he said.

"There are many more to tell," replied Ben.

"Keep on telling them," Capella said. Then he died. The gang could not stay in Rome. They escaped on a ship. But Nihilus was following them in another ship.

Later, on the ship, Helena told a story to Justin and Marcus.

Two friends of Jesus were walking to a village called Emmaus not far from Jerusalem. They were very sad. They were thinking about how Jesus had died.
Someone else joined them.
It was Jesus. But they did not recognize him.
"What are you talking about?" he asked.
This surprised them.

They told him that their leader, Jesus, had been killed by the Romans. But when two of their women friends went to his tomb it was empty. They were sad and puzzled. Jesus talked to them and they felt much better.

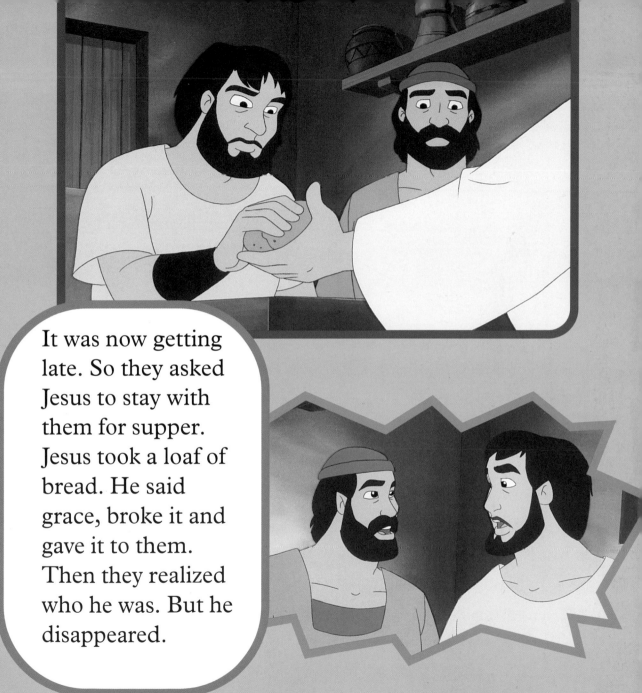

It was now getting late. So they asked Jesus to stay with them for supper. Jesus took a loaf of bread. He said grace, broke it and gave it to them. Then they realized who he was. But he disappeared.

The ship could not take
the gang all the way to a
safe place. They had to
walk through the sands.
They did not get far.
"Ah! So we meet
again," said a voice.
It was Nihilus!
A terrible fight began,
and soon Nihilus, Tacticus and Ben were
out of sight.

Zak, Helena and the children were left behind. "We've got to find Ben and Tacticus," said Zak. "But we have lost their tracks." Zak was downhearted. So Helena told a story about a friend of Jesus called Thomas.

The two disciples who met Jesus on the road came back. They told everyone that Jesus was alive.
"We know. Simon Peter saw him," everyone replied.

Later, Jesus appeared to his friends.
"Shalom! Peace be with you. Look
at my hands and my feet. It's me.
Touch me and you'll see. It's
true. I'm alive.

"Have you anything to eat?" he
asked.
Thomas was not there that time.
He wanted to see for himself.
"Unless I see the nail marks
on his hands and feet and
touch them and put my
hands in his side I won't
believe you," he said.
Suddenly, Jesus was
standing among them.
"Shalom! Peace be with
you."
He showed Thomas his
hands.
"My Lord and my God!" said Thomas.

While Tacticus
and Nihilus were
fighting, Nihilus
slipped over the
edge of the ravine.
Tacticus tried
to save him but
Nihilus fell to the
bottom.

When they ended their journey, there was a surprise for Marcus and Justin. Their parents were waiting for them. Tacticus and Miriam asked Anna if they could adopt her. They had a party and Ben told another two stories.

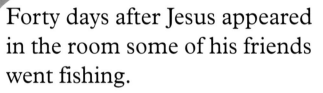

Forty days after Jesus appeared in the room some of his friends went fishing.
They fished all night and caught nothing. At dawn someone called to them from the shore to try again. It was Jesus.
Soon their nets were full of fish. "Simon Peter, look. It's Jesus!" said John. Peter rushed to Jesus through the waves.
Afterwards they cooked breakfast.

About six weeks later Jesus and his friends climbed a hill near Bethany. Jesus talked to the disciples. Suddenly a mist descended and Jesus was gone. They never saw him again. But they knew his death was not the end.

"And so it can be for us," said Ben. "Each one of us can be a storykeeper, even you, Marcus. Now you know stories about Jesus as a baby, the wonderful things he did and said. And as we pass on these stories many others come to know them, until one day there are as many storykeepers as there are stars in the sky."

The end ...